GSA FORM 3340 File Cover Sheet / Action Memorandum

W9-BKJ-250

FILE REVIEWED BY: DATE: AUG 05 1996

RECOMMENDED ACTION:

Bill - There's lots of memories here but I think we better get rid of this —

Hillary

FORWARD TO: The President

FILE REVIEWED BY: Bill   DATE: AUG 06 1996

RECOMMENDED ACTION:

George - I concur with Hillary. Let's deep six this stuff ASAP. Bill

FORWARD TO: Stephanapolons

FILE REVIEWED BY: G. STEPHANAPOLOUS   DATE: SEP 17 1996

RECOMMENDED ACTION: LEON — MY SHREDDER'S JAMMED. COULD YOU GET SOMEONE TO TAKE CARE OF THIS? BUT PLEASE, NOT THAT MORON WHO FOUND HILLARY'S LAW FIRM RECORDS ON HER BOOKSHELF. YOU KNOW, THE ONE HILLARY THREW HER SHOE AT? WHAT THE HELL IS HER NAME?

FORWARD TO: PANETTA   I REMEMBER! SELMA THURSTON!

FILE REVIEWED BY: Selma Thurston   DATE: SEP 18 1996

RECOMMENDED ACTION:

Put on tippy-top of big pile of papers on bookshelf. I sure hope no one finds it.

FORWARD TO:

THE WHITE H
WASHINGT

Bill –
Just finished going through
your dear departed mother's
safe deposit box. Here are the
items I think you were looking for.

Hillary

ORDER OF BIRTH RECORD

FOR USE WITH TWINS ONLY
NEWBORN IDENTIFICATION:
Twin Babies

8-19-45	*Fessenden*
DATE	DOCTOR

TYPE OF TWINS: Fraternal

GIVEN NAMES OF FIRSTBORN: William Jefferson Gingrich

TIME OF DELIVERY: 4:45 P.M.

8 lbs. 7 ozs.	**Male**
WEIGHT AT BIRTH	GENDER

COLOR OF EYES: Blue

GIVEN NAMES OF SECONDBORN: Newton Hamilton Gingrich

TIME OF DELIVERY: 5:25 P.M.

7 lbs. 11 ozs.	**Male**
WEIGHT AT BIRTH	GENDER

COLOR OF EYES: Brown

MOTHER'S MAIDEN NAME: Virginia Dell Cassidy

HUMBUG COUNTY HOSPITAL
HOGWASH, ARKANSAS

Miss Marie Purvis's School for Little Folk
Hope, Arkansas

Final Report Card for 3rd Grade

SYSTEM OF GRADING
A-EXCELLENT
B-GOOD
C-AVERAGE
D-BELOW AVERAGE
F-FAILING

ATTENDANCE & GROWTH	YEARLY AVERAGE	TEACHERS' COMMENT The space below will be used by the teachers when they feel there is need for additional comment
DAYS ABSENT	O	
DAYS TARDY	16	
READING	a	
ARITHMETIC	a	
RECITATION	a	
WRITING	a	
SPELLING	a	
CONDUCT	F	Must stop asking little girls if they "want to see my pee-pee"

Marie Purvis — Principal

Lydia Crevice — Teacher

Parent's Signature **Virginia Cassidy Clinton**

Summary of Year's Progress

Promoted to _____ Grade

Promoted to _____ Grade

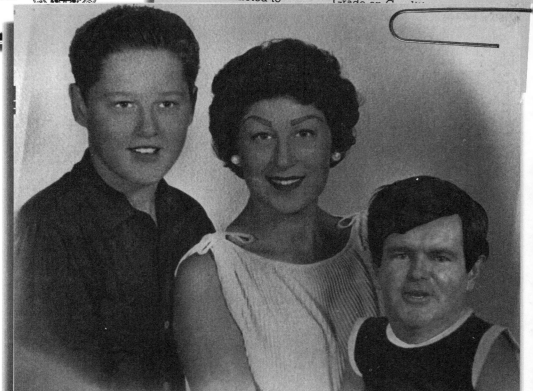

Hillary Rodham Grade 2

What I Would Do If I Were Queen Of America

If I were Queen of America I would make everybody happy, but only if they obeyed all my rules. Here are my rules.

1. Because I am smarter than everyone, I say what we're going to do, and no arguing or talking back or taking votes.

2. If somebody does something bad, then that person has to go and live in a room filled with bugs until I say they can come out, which may be never.

3. I say what's bad and what's not, but just because it's bad when you do it doesn't mean it's bad when I do it.

4. I get to look at what you're writing and if it's something bad about me you go to the bug room.

5. If I catch someone making faces behind my back, a doctor fixes it so their face stays like that forever.

6. When I break a rule or tell a lie it doesn't count because as Queen I have permanent double X-sies.

I think I would be a very good Queen of America, and I would have a King to help me run things, but I could take away his crown whenever I want. The End.

GIRL SCOUTS

July 22, 1957

Miss Hillary Rodham
62 Pocono Lane
Lake Winona, Pa. 18360

Dear Hillary,

I am surprised and a little saddened that you find selling Girl Scout cookies door-to-door "a demeaning and belittling activity that perpetuates hateful sex-based stereotypes."

Replacing this long-standing, universally recognized and much-beloved tradition with the explicitly profit-making "gender-neutral" Troop-oriented enterprises you have proposed, such as selling aluminum siding or marketing "Trooperware" brand plastic containers, would not only open the Girl Scouts to accusations that we are competing unfairly with local businesses, but would also transform a lighthearted and ladylike activity into what was essentially a money-grubbing enterprise.

I must also say that your suggestion that the Girl Scouts of America raise additional revenue by participating in leisure-oriented real estate developments centered around our campsites in rural areas or engaging in speculative investments in the Chicago commodities markets based on inside information collected by Scouts in bogus household "surveys" are in my view both inappropriate and improper and would fundamentally violate our historic tradition of personal integrity and selfless service to others.

In answer to your questions about our Personal Achievement Awards Program, the Girl Scouts do not presently offer Merit Badges in Issue Advocacy, Committee Formation, Protest Letter Composition, Handbill Distribution, Picket Line Establishment, or Boycott Coordination, and we have no plans to do so in the forseeable future.

In the hope that you may come to adopt a more supportive attitude towards our programs in the future, I've enclosed a copy of the recipe for our deluxe chocolate chip cookies. I can tell that you are a very determined young lady who will probably pursue a professional career, but believe me, you never know when the ability to bake up a really great dessert treat will come in handy.

Sincerely,

Clement K. Hornsby
Assistant to the National President

THE WHITE HOUSE

WASHINGTON

September 6, 1963

Miss Hillary Rodham
235 North Wisner Road
Park Ridge, Illinois

Dear Hillary,

How kind of you to write and encourage me to run against Jack for the Presidency next year. I'm sorry to say that I have made a firm decision to support my husband's bid for a second term, but I think if I had a few more supporters like you I would most certainly be a shoe-in!

To answer your interesting questions, no, I don't sit in on Cabinet meetings - I'm really much too busy with the daily demands of running this marvelous and fascinating house and arranging the President's demanding social schedule to have much time "to give those dumb old men a piece of my mind," as you so charmingly put it.

And as for your query about my role in the event of a Russian missile attack, I'm quite sure I lack authority as First Lady to order a retaliatory strike. However, I am not entirely without power in that area. You see, I've made it a rule that at formal White House dinners the nuclear launch codes are taken out of that tacky black suitcase that follows the President everywhere and put in a Louis Vuitton portmanteau.

Since I am not ready to throw my hat in the ring (and it's probably a good thing that I am not, because Oleg Cassini would be furious with me if I tossed one of his beautiful pillbox hats on a sofa, let alone into a political arena!), I do hope you will support my husband. While it is true that he has not appointed many women to high positions in his Administration, you can rest assured that the needs of members of the fair sex are never far from his mind.

Very truly yours,

Jacqueline Kennedy

Jacqueline Kennedy

Date: September 23, 1968

To: Hillary Rodham
Stone-Davis Hall
Wellesley College
Wellesley, Mass. 02181

SDS
STUDENTS FOR A
DEMOCRATIC SOCIETY

Dear Weathergirl —

Congratulations on successfully completing Weather Underground
Summer Camp! Below is your personal evaluation by your Senior
Struggle Leader.

BOMB-MAKING:
Good grasp of basic concept of explosives, wiring, timer, etc. Needs
work on assembly and placement of device for maximum effect.

HAND-TO-HAND COMBAT:
Excellent use of feet for groin kick. Also best in class on silent
approach for knife in back.

AGITATION & PROPAGANDA:
Superb speaker, natural-born liar. Extremely effective at
manipulating crowds as well as one-on-one deception.

ESCAPE & EVASION:
First-rate ability to totally alter appearance and change
character but has to get rid of glasses — wonky look is dead
giveaway!

DRUG PRODUCTION:
Lacks "green thumb" - all marijuana plants died. Also, not cut out to
be a chemist - LSD batch produced only mild laxative effect. Came in
last in magic brownie bake-off.

RECOMMENDED REVOLUTIONARY ROLE:
Destroy system from within.

Burn after reading! (Use American flag to start fire).
Power to the people!

Attested To By
Kathy Boudin

Kathy Boudin

Yale University *New Haven, Connecticut 06520*

OFFICE OF ADMISSIONS
LAW SCHOOL
401A Yale Station

April 13, 1969

Miss Hillary Rodham
Stone-Davis Hall
Wellesley College
Wellesley, Mass. 02181

Dear Miss Rodham,

The Admissions Committee has concluded its meetings, and I am pleased to advise you that your application for Admission to the Law School has been accepted. Congratulations and welcome to the Class of 1972.

I'd like to take this opportunity to thank you for having gone to the trouble of pointing out the grammatical errors in our application form, particularly our misuse of "affect" for "effect" and "which" for "that" in the entry which asked candidates to enumerate "any other considerations which might effect our decision." Your helpful corrections will be incorporated into next year's version.

I also feel I would be remiss if I did not commend the superb paper you submitted as your Writing Sample. Your articulate and well-researched presentation of the hypothetical multimillion-dollar antidiscrimination suit which could be brought against Yale by a fully qualified female applicant who was rejected when male candidates of similar abilities gained admission was most impressive indeed.

I do not know whether you have applied to other law schools, but if you have, I do hope that the fact that both Harvard and Stanford are invariably rated ahead of Yale in quality of instruction and have consistently demonstrated a far better record of placing their graduates in high-paying jobs in top law firms and in prestigious positions in government service will not in any way effect your decision about which institution to attend.

And although I must concede that New Haven, with its serious crime problem, substandard housing, and utter dearth of basic urban amenities cannot in any way compete with the idyllic living conditions in Cambridge and Palo Alto, we would certainly regret losing you to one of our clearly superior sister schools. Incidentally, I'd like to go on record as saying that the reports of cholera in the city water supply are inaccurate.

We are grateful for your interest in the Law School, but please be assured that if you elect to pursue your legal studies at one of our more highly regarded competitors, we would certainly understand the reasons for your choice.

Sincerely yours,

Harris Twill
Assistant Dean

Dear **THRILLARY —**

It's hard to believe the piggies' favorite holiday has rolled around again, but here we are with only a few more "chopping days" left til Christmas, or Man'sSon'sMess which was the way we always celebrated it back at the Spahn Ranch. All us girls used to get together to sing a few of the carols Charlie wrote like "Deck the halls with blood for Charlie", and then Tex and Clem would go out and kill a Christmas turkey (or just an ordinary jerk!), and we'd get one of the really big maryjane plants from out back and decorate it with bones and bullets and bent nails and Buck knives on those little thong things and put a gold Swastika on top.

Well, it's been quite a year. You probably heard by now about how the whole Pig Establishment is plotting ways to pin a lot of murders on the Family. It's a scream. Just like Charlie predicted, they are trying to make us out as some kind of mad dog devil killer fiend lepers, when in fact we are just full of love for everyone, though right now not for Sadie Glutz who should learn to keep her mouth shut or she won't find shelter from Helter Skelter.

But let's not dwell here on the negative, because Charlie says that just gets in the way of our mission which is to instill fear into the pigs, but a loving kind of fear, and bring on judgment day which is here now for all, and anyway I know what you want and that is News! so here goes.

LuLu had the flu pretty bad last spring, but she got over it, and Crystal got kind of burned on her elbow doing up a batch of tie-dyed stuff, but Charlie made it all well. Gypsy and Cupid had a romance, and then Gypsy thought she was pregnant, and we had some fun thinking of baby names like Tripsy if it was a girl and Stupid if it was a boy, only she just missed her period. Katie came up with a great new recipe for these little LSD lemondrop things she calls acid rock candy, and Zero shot himself to death playing Russian roulette in November, and Capistrano and Little Patty and Country Sue were there, and so was Bruce, anyway Charlie says these things happen and it's according to a plan, only we can't see it.

Sandy, Ouisch, Cathy, and Mary and me are still on the "outside" so to speak, and we're all here for Charlie, and we'll be here for him forever, and we hope you will be too (or else!). That's all for now, and I'm going to close on a happy note, which is to say what Charlie told us, and that is to always think of the Now — No time to look back — No time to say how.

Charlie sends his special love to you and to all the other absent members of the Family, and to the piggies he says, have a Scary Christmas and get ready for a really Crappy New Year when He lights fires in your cities with His thoughts!

SQUEAKY

2 December 1969

Mr. Bill Clinton
46 Leckford Road
Oxford, OX1 3GB

Dear Mr. Bill Clinton,

I am responding on behalf of the Ambassador to your letter of 12th November inquiring about the possibility of becoming a Swedish citizen.

Right off the base-ball bat as you Americans say, let me thank you for your kind words about the country of Sweden. Yes, it is true we have not invaded anybody for a very long time, and I am sure we have no plans to do so any time soon! I also agree that our furniture combines so nicely both beauty and comfort and good price, although it is maybe the Danish modern design that you are thinking of. The Marimekko fabrics are indeed most striking, but in point of fact they are actually Finnish (this too is a common confusion). I would heartfully concur that Mr. Ingmar Bergman is a fine filmmaker, but I must correct one misimpression - Miss Ingrid Bergman is not his daughter. Also, unless her telephone number is publicly listed, I could not of course provide it even if I had it. I most certainly wish I did! (This is a small joke which I am making.)

In reply to your other inquiries, firstly, since Sweden is a kingdom, we do not have a President, so you see no one can become one, not even a 100% Swedish man! (It is Finland, a republic, up with which again you are perhaps mixing us). Secondly, under our law, only a child with at least one Swedish parent is qualified to sit in the Parliament and thusly to be eligible to be Prime Minister, but foreign born personages who settle in Sweden can serve in many capacities, including for example as a Stengsforsst, which is a type of animal control officer but also with responsibility for handling certain traffic infractions, or as a member of a Board, such as the Fish Purity Board or the Beet Roundtable.

At this present time, there is to my own personal knowledge not a MacDonald restaurant in Sweden, but I think you would enjoy the very excellent and most delectable Swedish meatballs which are indeed a meal in themself. And certainly our justly famous Smorgasbord buffets are nothing at which to be sneezing!

In closing, may I say that I am confident that my fellow landsmen will happily extend the warm hand of welcome should you decide to bid farewell to the place of your birth and settle in our beloved and beautiful Sweden, which by the way does not have fjords - that is Norway.

Very truly yours,

Sven Carlsson

Sven Carlsson
First Secretary

Church of the Universal and Transcendant Spirit, Inc.

Certificate of Ordination

Let it be known by all our beloved brethren throughout the land that

Reverend William Jefferson Clinton

having been examined and found to be of the highest moral character and spiritual probity, and having stated in writing that he has heard a sacred calling to holy orders, and having further acknowledged and accepted this holy summons by delivering into my hands a certified check in the sum of **$75.00**, is hereby consecrated and confirmed as a

Junior Minister of the Divine Truth

with all the privileges and responsibilities appurtenant thereunto, including the right of exemption from taxation **{Senior Ministers Only}** and the solemn duty as a member of our clergy to refuse to engage in any form of military service, whether combatant or not, or to submit to conscription, such acts being directly contrary to the deeply held convictions and fundamental doctrines of this duly established and constitutionally protected Church.

In witness whereof, I have hereunder affixed my signature and seal on this _9th_ day of _September_ in the year of our Lord _1969_. at my ecclesiastical seat at P.O. Box 26085, Burbank, California.

Vernon T. Snellgrove

SUPREME HIGH BISHOP OF THE PACIFIC DIOCESE

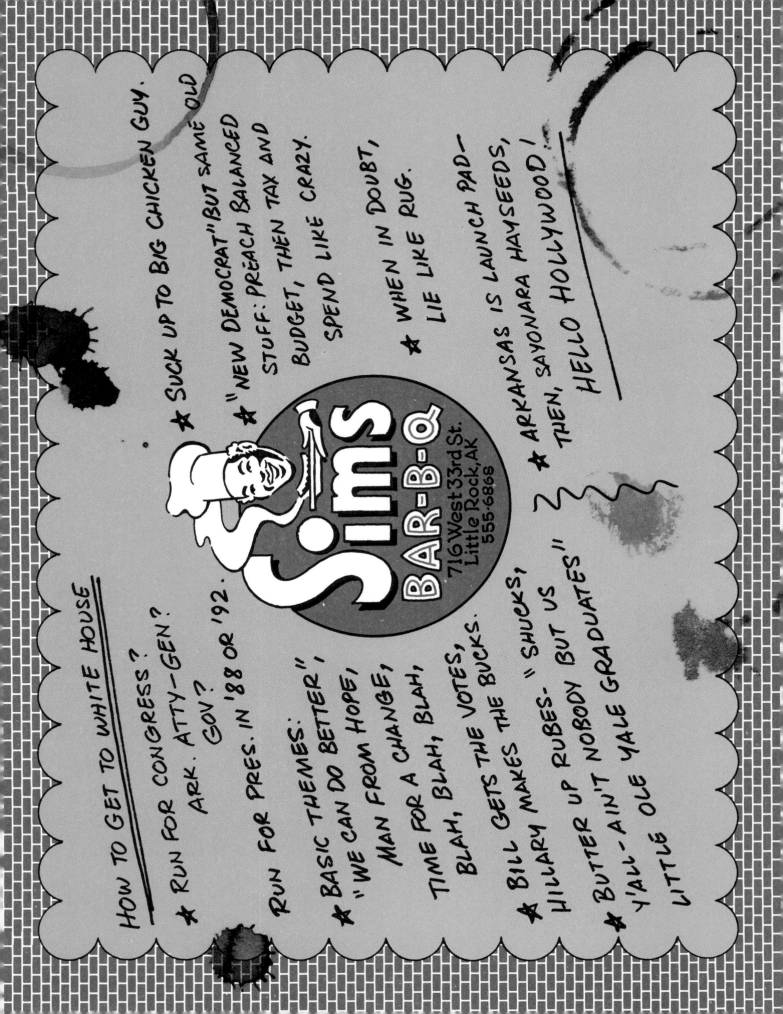

HOW TO GET TO WHITE HOUSE

* RUN FOR CONGRESS?
  ARK. ATTY-GEN?
  GOV?

RUN FOR PRES. IN '88 OR '92.

* BASIC THEMES:
  "WE CAN DO BETTER",
  "MAN FROM HOPE,
  TIME FOR A CHANGE,
  BLAH, BLAH, BLAH,
  BILL GETS THE VOTES,
  HILLARY MAKES THE BUCKS.

* BUTTER UP RUBES- "SHUCKS,
  Y'ALL-AIN'T NOBODY BUT US
  LITTLE OLE YALE GRADUATES"

* SUCK UP TO BIG CHICKEN GUY.

* "NEW DEMOCRAT"BUT SAME OLD
  STUFF: PREACH BALANCED
  BUDGET, THEN TAX AND
  SPEND LIKE CRAZY.

* WHEN IN DOUBT,
  LIE LIKE RUG.

* ARKANSAS IS LAUNCH PAD—
  THEN, SAYONARA HAYSEEDS,
  HELLO HOLLYWOOD!

Sims BAR-B-Q
716 West 33rd St.
Little Rock, AK
555-6868

Tyson Foods, Inc. P.O. Box 2020 • Springdale, AR 72765-2020 • Phone (501) 290-4000

May 16, 1983

Governor Bill Clinton
The Governor's Mansion
1800 Center Street
Little Rock, Ark. 72206

Dear Governor,

Dale asked me to drop you a line and say thank you very kindly indeed for helping us out with that there truck weight thing? All of us here are real appreciative of what you done for us, and we'd sure like to show our gratitude but no way would we try to give you anything that wasn't one-hundred percent proper and above-board and all?

Well, sir, Dale and I got to talking, and he said well, heck, the time they must spend with all the legislating and vetoing and sending out writs of hocus-pocus and so forth and so on, I bet they don't have a minute to spare to go through the newspapers the way ordinary folk do and cut out the coupons we put in there every day that let you save two bits off a package of our plump drumsticks or give you a two-for-one on a nice frier or some good deal like that?

And so when you come right down to it, what we figured is you all have been missing out on something everybody else gets and in point of fact all we are trying to do right here is just make up for something that is owed you, if you follow my way of thinking?

Anyway, we really put our heads together on this thing, and the way we worked it out, you are entitled to a whole lot of discounts on pretty near a ton of our chicken, but maybe it would be easier if we could sort of make that up to you by sending you and the little lady one big coupon that took the place of all them nickel and dime sized daily coupons you would have clipped if you'd of had the time to clip them which you being so hard-working you didn't?

I do believe that about sums it up. Now, Dale told me special to be sure to ask you to send his best to your missus, and I will conclude here by doing just that, and you take care of yourself, too, you hear?

Your friend,

Billy Joe Gallus

Billy Joe Gallus
Director of Marketing

THIS COUPON GOOD FOR
$100,000
OFF ALL FINE TYSON PRODUCTS
*MAYBE REDEEMED FOR
FULL CASH VALUE*
NO EXPIRATION DATE

ROSE LAW FIRM

A PROFESSIONAL ASSOCIATION

ATTORNEYS

120 EAST FOURTH STRE

LITTLE ROCK, ARKANSAS 7

TELEPHONE (501) 555-913

TELECOPIER (501) 555-130

B. B. ROSE
1826-1963

July 14, 1987

A tropical vacation paradise where Arkansas says Aloha!

Ms. Hillary Rodham
The Governor's Mansion
1800 Center Street
Little Rock, AR 72201

Dear Hillary:

I've reviewed the photocopy you sent ov
proposed Whitewater sales brochure. I thi
and it really grabs you, though I must say
loved the previous version with that descr
flower-bedecked hills and lush vineyards w
kissed by the balmy Mediterranean sunshin
"Les Ozarques."

Needless to say, the old fuddies here
liberties you need to take writing sell
marketing a turkey like this property. A
agree that somewhere down the road there
fuss about false advertising or some bul
legal opinion from us going on record as
in case there's ever a problem. With al
showed the brochure to LeRoy in the mail
not what you'd call a fast reader or any
liked the pretty picture a whole lot, a
heard him make the following unequivoca
quote, "It sure looks mighty nice to me" unquote, so as
far as I'm concerned, you can say, under oath if necessary, that it was
"examined by someone at the law firm who stated that it seemed fine to
him."

If this new brochure doesn't do the job, then I'd say go ahead with
your plan to have the Arkansas Department of Education buy the land with
$500,000 in child nutrition subsidy funds and divide it into one-inch-
size pieces and enclose deeds in the little cereal boxes they give out
in the school breakfast program.

With best regards, I am,

Sincerely yours,

WEBSTER L. HUBBELL

WLH: hnb

Encl.

NEW WORLD ORDER
FORMERLY THE ONE-WORLD CONSPIRACY

PARTICIPATING ORGANIZATIONS:
• ASPEN INSTITUTE • BILDERBERG SOCIETY • COUNCIL ON FOREIGN RELATIONS • FORD FOUNDATION
• GENERAL AGREEMENT ON TRADE & TARIFFS • INTERNATIONAL MONETARY FUND
• RENAISSANCE WEEKENDS, INC. • TRILATERAL COMMISSION • UNITED NATIONS • WORLD BANK

August 7, 1989

Governor Bill Clinton & Hillary Rodham Clinton
The Governor's Mansion
1800 Center Street
Little Rock, Arkansas 72206

Dear Bill and Hillary,

I am delighted to inform you that you have been selected by the "powers that be" to win the Presidency of the United States in 1992. For appearances sake, we do like to "go through the motions" of your quaint American democratic procedures, so I think it would be best if you delayed the announcement of your candidacy until late in 1991.

I must say that the presentation the two of you made to our little group in Baden-Baden this June was one of the most effective I have ever seen (and, remember, I have been around long enough to have been present for John Kennedy's legendary performance in 1959!). I can tell you that the voting wasn't even close. Mr. Bush only received support from the old Skull & Bones crowd and, of course, Queen Elizabeth. Even Henry Kissinger went with you! And the Pope! I was most impressed!

On a somewhat more serious note, may I take this opportunity to remind you that the commitments you made to the Organization, including, among others, the speedy enactment of NAFTA, the placement of U.S. troops under United Nations command, and the reappointment of Alan Greenspan as Chairman of the Federal Reserve, are to be taken with the utmost seriousness? I don't think I need to make mention of the price that Richard Nixon paid for his little "rebellion" from our dictates in 1973.

As you know, our shadowy organization of international bankers operates a worldwide network of highly placed individuals who stand ready to assist you. Please do not hesitate to avail yourself of the services of members of our American auxillary at any time, including Charles Allen, Adm. William Crowe, Lloyd Cutler, David Gergen, Sen. Albert Gore, Don Hewitt at *60 Minutes*, Michael Ovitz, and of course, Ross Perot.

Sincerely yours,

Bernhard

Prince Bernhard of the Netherlands
Chairman

P.S. It would be most helpful if you could signal your acceptance of these terms and your allegiance to our brotherhood by appearing in public on any occasion of your chosing wearing the ceremonial "duck hat" headgear given to you on the night of your initiation.

from the everlovin' desk of: JAMES CARVILLE, Stupid!

Bill, Hillary -

O.K., guys, first the good news -
I got the negatives and all other
copies of these photos from Mary
Matalin.

The bad news is, I had to trade her
the picture of George Bush as V.P.
playing horseshoes with Saddam
Hussein and that great candid shot
of Dan Quayle in a ballgown on
Malcolm Forbes's yacht.

Also, I have to marry her.

Jimbo

Jimbo

BLOODWORTH/THOMASON
MOZARK
P R O D U C T I O N S

January 24, 1993

Dear Hillary,

Just a quick note to say thanks for your incredibly sweet words about how professionally the Inaugural festivities were produced. We went all out to make the celebration something very special, and we're just tickled to death that everything was such a smash. And we just want to say again what a pleasure and a privilege it is to work for two such great friends and terrific people!

Hillary, can we bring up a little problem that you could really help us with? At the MTV ball we had a chance to talk with Bill for a couple of minutes (between saxophone sets!) and an offhand remark he made really sounded to us like he was beginning to back away from his commitment to allow gays in the military.

We'll let you in on a secret. We've made a <u>very</u> succesful pitch to Universal for a new situation comedy tentatively titled "Privates" about three openly gay career soldiers in an army unit in Georgia - it's sort of a Bilko in drag or "Fruit Troop." John Ritter, Steve Guttenberg, and John Stamos have all showed a lot of interest in the project. (We're also thinking of semi-regular status for Roger Clinton as a Forrest Gump/Gomer Pyle running character who's on permanent K.P.)

Just about the only negative we've run into is due to a current trend at the studios to shift their TV focus towards "reality-based" comedy as opposed to fantasy themes, like families of space aliens. Frankly, we heard a lot of scepticism that the President would actually make good on his campaign promise to change Defense Department policy banning uncloseted homosexuals from serving. Hence, some real doubts about the piece's "facticality" - how's that for Hollywood jargon?

A good clear statement early on from Bill that he's sticking to his guns on this issue would definitely put us over the top on this one. And, hey, it's the right thing to do.

By the way, the name of that L.A.-based hair stylist you asked about for Bill is Christophe. He charges 200 bucks for a haircut, but who's to know?

We'll be back in D.C. on the 30th if the White House Travel Office doesn't screw up our reservations again. What a bunch of clowns!

Love ya,

Harry + Linda
Harry and Linda

Bill - Let's throw them a bone and go with the gay thing. —Hillary

KAKI HOCKERSMITH INTERIORS
5116 Kavanaugh Boulevard
Little Rock, Arkansas 72207

February 16, 1993

Mrs. Hillary Rodham Clinton
First Lady of the United States
The White House
1600 Pennsylvania Ave. NW
Washington, D.C. 20500

Dear Mrs. Clinton,

I'm enclosing the sample of the proposed stencil for the seal of the First Lady. As we discussed, this new design would be embroidered with the existing Presidential seal in an alternating pattern on the 3,000 yards of burgundy-apricot satin-backed tasseled velour cloth for the window treatments in the proposed redecoration of the Oval Office.

As you requested, I have obtained a very rough preliminary estimate for reconstructing the Oval Office into a heart-shape. I'd say we're looking at $9,500,000, give or take a million, and another $750,000 for acquisition of those unique reproduction antique pieces we talked about, including the Shaker Paper Mangle, the Louis XVI Dossier-Pulverisateur, the Chippendale Correspondence Thresher, the Sheraton Dispatch Cutter, the Duncan Phyfe Document Chopper, and the Tiffany Missive Slicer.

I'll have a sample in a week or so of that off-white creamy-eggshell all-weather paint for the exterior of the White House. It may be a little bit controversial at first, but I just know everyone will end up loving it!

Best wishes,

Kaki

Kaki

PROPOSED
DESIGN FOR THE
SEAL OF THE
FIRST LADY OF
OF THE
UNITED STATES

| SECRET "MAXIMUM" HEALTH CARE PLAN | Meeting with First Lady 3-2-93

"Go-for-broke" approach— may have to water down

✱ KEY POINTS ✱

• Best way to keep costs in line → get rid of oldsters (75+ yrs?) Fed program to provide Senior Citizen Centers with scary movies, tricky-to-use power tools. Kevorkian for Surgeon General ?

• Draft all docs— you ~~can~~ want to practice medicine, got to join Public Health Service. (Get Doogie Howser, hunks from E.R. to endorse idea?)

• Put everybody's I.Q. on health I.D. card. Dummies get placebos, risky new surgery, M.D.s and hospitals with bad records, psycho nurses. A+ types get A+ care.

• Enforce good health ~~habits~~ habits— put metered Stairmasters in every home. Inspector checks every month to make sure you're getting workout.

• Social Value Assessments ("Defend Your Life" type hearings) by Community Service Boards determines who gets scarce organs, expensive procedures. Bad guys (polluters, greedy developers, etc.) bite banana.

• If program produces long waits for operations (like in ~~Britan~~ Britain, Canada), give out free copies of "The Little Engine That Could."

• Pay for program with "fun fee" dollar-a-ticket tax on all sports events— NFL, NBA, NHL, baseball, boxing, Indy 500, etc.
(Olympics exempt?)

✱ ~~Also~~ Also, 10% "leisure tax" on video rentals, fishing tackle, motor boats, hunting rifles, lift tickets, pasta makers, gardening equipment, hot tubs, pool toys & teddy bears, plus big "fat tax" on candy bars, milk shakes, salty snacks, french fries and beer. (No tax on BBQ or greens fees— Pres will nix)

CGE011493

Department of Defense

Office of the Secretary of Defense

MEMORANDUM TO: Hillary Clinton

FROM: Secretary Les Aspin   *L.a.*

DATE: April 30, 1993

RE: Names for Warships

First of all, I want to thank you again for your visit to the Pentagon and your wonderful speech to the Joint Armed Forces Wives. Mrs. Powell was especially grateful for your thoughtful remarks about General Powell.

As you requested, I have done some thinking about your suggestion to name the two nuclear-powered aircraft carriers now under construction at the Pascagoula Shipyards the USS EDITH WHARTON (CVN-70) and the USS HARRIET TUBMAN (CVN-71).

I must say frankly that I think those designations would be a mistake. I would readily agree that both of these women were persons of great note in American history and are certainly deserving of national recognition. I also concede that there is a precedent for honoring Americans whose achievements lay outside the military sphere in the past practice of naming Polaris and Poseidon missile submarines for outstanding literary figures like Ralph Waldo Emerson and Henry David Thoreau.

Nevertheless, I feel stongly that given the fact that we have "rocked the boat" pretty hard in the last couple of months over gays in the military and women serving in combat roles, we should try to avoid doing anything that further sours our relations with senior military officers, particularly when it's easily avoidable. In that regard, I can say absolutely that the Chiefs would go "ballistic" if this course of action were pursued.

Incidentally, at the time of the President's visit to USS THEODORE ROOSEVELT (CVN-66) in March of this year, I mentioned in passing that there was a great deal of sentiment at the Pentagon for naming the first of the new carriers for Ronald Reagan, and that a generous gesture like that would not only earn us points with the Pentagon brass but also yield a big political payoff. The President stated that he believed that was an excellent idea, and added lightheartedly (I think!) that he would like to name the other one for Elvis Presley.

On that other matter, please let Al Gore know that we finally found his court-martial records. I'm pretty sure there are no copies. The originals have been disposed of.

Could you also tell the President that I checked with the Secretary of the Army and he says he can't authorize sending the West Point football squad to play alongside the University of Arkansas Razorbacks in the forthcoming Fiesta Bowl because there's no way he can figure out to justify it as a legitimate training exercise. Sorry about that.

Bill — I want Aspin fired now! —Hillary

HRC — I agree 100%! Bill

MEMORANDUM

OFFICE OF THE BROTHER OF THE PRESIDENT
WASHINGTON

To: The President

From: Roger Clinton *R.C.*

Subject: My hilarious new comedy material - Redneck President jokes!

Hey Bubba! I'm putting together a great new act for a kind of cabaret show at the "K" Street Komedy Klub right here in good ole D.C., so I thought I oughta run some of my "better" stuff by you.

You Know You're a Redneck President When —

— the Congress threatens to send you a bill you don't like, and you say "go right ahead because I ain't going to pay it!"

— you drop by the Bureau of Alcohol, Tobacco, and Firearms to drink some whiskey, smoke a cigar, and kill some deer!

— you can't spell any of the places you invade!

— you begin your State of the Union speech by saying, "I don't know about the State of the Union, but the Confederacy is doin' just fine!"

— you always thought Federal Reserve was a brand of bourbon!

— you think debate is what goes on da hook!

— you call the Department of Defense and tell them to round up some barbed wire to build you a hog pen!

I got a million of these! By the way, can I borrow your spare saxophone?

Hillary — Help!

Bill — With talent like this, Roger really is ready for a world tour. I think if we put our own people in the travel office, they can handle it. — Hillary

WORLD**WIDE**TRAVEL, INC.

2228 Cottondale Lane
Little Rock, Arkansas 72202

*"Handling All the White House's
Travel Needs Since Late Last Week"*

---

20 MAY 1993

MS. CATHERINE CORNELIUS
WHITE HOUSE TRAVEL OFFICE
WASHINGTON DC 20500

PROPOSED ITINERARY/ROGER CLINTON WORLD CONCERT TOUR (1ST LEG)

DATE	CITY-AIRPORT	TIME	AIRLINE	FLT	SEAT
25MAY	LV DC/DULLES	745AM	AMERICAN	971	30F
TUE	AR BELIZE	1258PM			

25MAY	HOTEL INFORMATION	GOAT BAY BEACH RESORT
TUE		66 MONKEY WALK
		BELIZE CITY, BELIZE
		1 ROOM - 7 NIGHTS
		CONF. # DESMOND21MAY

BOOKING INFORMATION   CLUB HOWZZAT?

      21B DEADMAN'S ALLEY
      BELIZE CITY SOUTH
      6 PERFS - 8 PM SHOWTIME
      CONTACT: CHUCKY
      OTHER PERFORMERS:
      BAD BOY ALL FIRED UP

2JUN	LV BELIZE	630AM	BRIT. AIRWAYS	255	51J
TUE	AR FALKLANDS	1155PM			

2JUN	HOTEL INFORMATION	MRS. WIGGINGS COTTAGES
TUE		NUMBER 7, THE ROAD
		STANLEY, FALKLAND ISLES
		1 ROOM - 5 NIGHTS
		CONF #: 1

BOOKING INFORMATION   YE OLDE PIG & THISTLE

      NUMBER 21, THE ROAD
      STANLEY, FALKLAND ISLES
      5 PERFS - 6 PM SHOWTIME
      CONTACT: GORD
      OTHER PERFORMERS:
      CLOGDANCE FESTIVAL

NOTE: LITTLE AMERICA BASE IN ANTARTICA WOULD LOVE TO HAVE ROGER COME
IN ON 8 JUNE TO DO A FEW SHOWS BUT SNOWS ARRIVE SOON AND THERE IS
RISK HE COULD BE TRAPPED THERE ALL WINTER. PLEASE ADVISE.

TOP SECRET

Washington, D.C. 20535

May 22, 1993

This we don't need

MEMORANDUM TO: THE PRESIDENT

FROM: DIRECTOR WILLIAM SESSIONS *WS*

SUBJECT: BACKGROUND CHECKS

In response to Mr. MacLarty's request, we instituted a full-field investigation of current Cabinet members to determine if any of them has a "nanny problem" that might become public knowledge at a later date.

One Cabinet Officer - Donna Shalala - does in fact have a nanny problem, although it is has a somewhat different dimension from the ones encountered by Ms. Zoe Baird and Judge Kimba Wood. Ms. Shalala did not employ an illegal alien as a nanny - she was one.

Donna Shalala's real name is Ladonna Consuela. She is a Honduran national who entered the U.S. with false documentation sometime in late 1952 or early 1953. She worked from March 1953 until May 1955 in the household of an elderly couple in Pittsburgh.

Although Ms. Shalala subsequently demonstrated remarkable dedication and intellectual powers in thoroughly mastering the English language and going on to earn advanced educational degrees, ultimately becoming the President of a prestigious college, her citizenship status has never been regularized.

And while we are on the subject of aliens, another Cabinet Officer has a potential problem, albeit one that is unrelated to the hiring of illegal immigrants to perform household duties.

The Bureau has come into possession of strong evidence that Secretary of State Warren Christopher is a being from another planet.

In addition to sworn statements from several State Dept. employees that Mr. Christopher is able to read minds, see through dense masonry walls and make small objects hover, we have testimony from two members of his personal staff that he seems to require substantial amounts of molybdenum (2 to 3 kilograms daily) as an essential part of his nutritional intake and when cut, bleeds a vivid green fluid that glows briefly before evaporating.

We have also intercepted unusual transmissions of beams of hyperluminal tachyon particles apparently emanating from the top floor of the State Department that we believe are directed at Bellatrix, a star in the constellation of Orion situated approximately 470 light years from Washington, D.C. Moreover, a court-approved wiretap of Secretary Christopher's home telephone has produced recordings of twenty-two conversations in a language which I can best describe as a cross between a barbershop quartet and a car alarm.

Finally, a routine sweep of Secretary Christopher's office on 9 May to locate possible eavesdropping devices revealed that what looked like an ordinary travel alarm clock on his desk in fact contained a functioning 10-megawatt fission-type nuclear reactor approximately the size of a cufflink connected to a microminiaturized transmitter which Bureau engineers calculate has the broadcasting power of a commercial television station.

Please advise what action you wish taken in regard to these matters.

7 June 1993

to mr. bill clinton u.s.a. president
whitehouse, washington, d-c
by special diplomatic courier

my dear mr. u.s.a. president clinton,

i am being directed by president yeltsin to have sended to you this photographical image which was in most recent week discovered in archives of k.g.b.

president yeltsin is asking to me to say he presents this to you sir with his kind compliments but also you please should remember that now you are owing to him a debt very big time.

he is also telling me to inform to you that name of girl with sizeable hooters who translates for russian ambassador is tatiana semenyovna but forget it she is well-known ball-demolisher.

warmed regards,

Vladimir Kuznetsov

vladimir kuznetsov
confidential secretary to the president

GRUPO MUCHO FRAUDULENTO DE MEXICO, S.A.

DOMICILIO SOCIAL: México, D.F.

DURACION: Noventa y nueve años

$20,000,000,000 M.N.

Capital Social: $ 6,550,000,000,000,000,000.00 M.N.

AMPARA

200 ACCIONES

TITULO No.
056407208

El portador representa DOSCIENTAS ACCIONES comunes de Usuarios de la Serie "F" del Grupo Mucho Fraudulento de México, Sociedad Anónima, con valor nominal de $1000.00 (Mil Pesos) Moneda Nacional, cada una, de las 500,000 acciones en que se divide el Capital Social

Grupo Mucho Fraudulento de México, Sociedad Anónima, se constituyó mediante gada ante el Notario Público No. 12 del Distrito Federal, señor Malvado Enc la Propiedad y de Comercio del Distrito Federal, bajo el No. 7, a fojas 18, vol sas modificaciones, la última de las cuales se protocolizó ante el mismo Notario en el Registro Particular de la Propiedad y de Comercio del Distrito Federal,

México, D.F., a 30 de novie

Embustero Tunante

Embustero Tunante
CONSEJERO

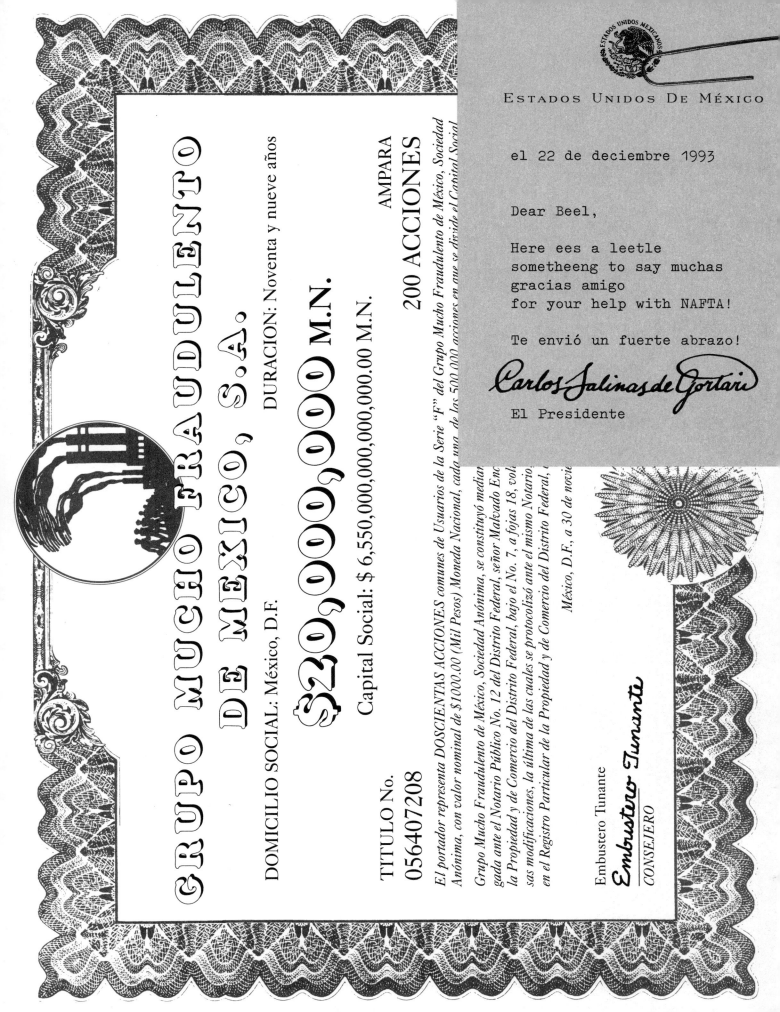

ESTADOS UNIDOS DE MÉXICO

el 22 de deciembre 1993

Dear Beel,

Here ees a leetle
sometheeng to say muchas
gracias amigo
for your help with NAFTA!

Te envió un fuerte abrazo!

Carlos Salinas de Gortari

El Presidente

DEPARTMENT OF THE INTERIOR

TO: THE PRESIDENT

FROM: SECRETARY BABBITT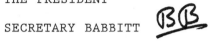

I'm enclosing a rough computer simulation of how the Mount
Rushmore National Memorial would look with the additional faces.

The cost of chiseling your image and that of the First Lady onto
the mountainside would be about $75 million. We could cover this
with a 1,000 % increase in fees for grazing and mineral extrac-
tion on public lands in the West - sort of appropriate if you
ask me since those ranchers and miners are all a bunch of chis-
elers anyway.

The Geological Survey inspected the rock wall adjacent to the
Lincoln sculpture - it's sound and stable, and there's no risk
at all of damaging the existing Borglund stonework when we jack-
hammer your likenesses into the adjacent area. However, I'd sug-
gest we put out some story that we found a hidden fault in the
cliff face, then drape the affected portion of the mountainside
in plastic sheeting for "urgent repairs" during the time it takes
to complete the job. At the end of your second term, presto! off
comes the tarp, and you're history!

Thanks again for keeping me in mind for that Supreme Court seat!

Central Intelligence Agency
Office of the Director

April 3, 1994

MEMORANDUM FROM THE DIRECTOR

FOR THE PRESIDENT'S EYES ONLY

RAW INTELLIGENCE DATA - DO NOT DISSEMINATE

SITUATION REPORT ON OPERATION HOUND DOG HUNT

Mr. President:

Acting per your instructions, I requested Port-au-Prince Chief of Station Ron
Barrett to send Agent "Hummingbird" into the hilly backlands in Haiti's Haute-
Terre Province to follow up on rumors of a local voodoo figure named "Lélévis" who
is said to bear a remarkable resemblance to the late (presumbably) Elvis Presley.

Operating under the cover of a Peace Corps medical volunteer, Hummingbird, who is
a fluent speaker of the local Creole language, eventually succeeded in overcoming
the naturally suspicious and reticent nature of the inhabitants of this extremely
secluded and primitive region of Haiti, and after some weeks in the area was able
to procure an invitation to a voodoo ceremony attended by "Lélévis."

According to Hummingbird, "Lélévis" was an enormously fat Caucasian male dressed
in a '70s-era Las Vegas-style sequinned outfit. Although he appeared to be in a
trance, he was clearly alive, and at one point he sang several bars of a song in
English that Hummingbird identified as "Heartbreak Hotel."

Showing remarkable resourcefulness, Hummingbird not only obtained a photograph of
the subject by using a camera concealed in a stethoscope, but also secured permis-
sion to treat a minor cut on the right index finger of "Lélévis" and thereby collected a sufficient amount of tissue and blood for later DNA comparison with
authenticated samples of Mr. Presley's hair in the possession of the Agency.

The results of these matching tests were received yesterday. With a 99.97% degree
of probability, the Haitian voodoo figure known as "Lélévis" is in fact Elvis
Presley. A review of our own files on Mr. Presley as well as additional documentation provided to us on your orders by the F.B.I. reveals that in the months before
his "death," Mr. Presley had in fact become interested in voodoo and actually con-
sulted with a voodoo "priest" named "Titi." Although on their face the facts of
this case do seem to strain credulity, we can only conclude that Mr. Presley's
body was somehow reanimated and transported to Haiti around the time of his
"funeral" in August of 1977.

In response to your hypothetical scenario of what might be required to "rescue"
Mr. Presley if this sighting were to be substantiated, let me, as a sort of foot-
note, quote agent Hummingbird, who has personal experience of the terrain and the
populace. The last line of his report read: "You'd need to send in the whole U.S.
Army to get him out of there."

National Aeronautics and
Space Administration

Headquarters
Washington, DC 20546-0001

FOR: THE PRESIDENT

FROM: HUBBLE SPACE TELESCOPE IMAGING CENTER

ENCLOSED PLEASE FIND PHOTOGRAPH ACQUIRED AT 23:45 G.M.T 16
AUGUST 1995 DURING ORBITAL PASSAGE OVER SOUTH OF FRANCE.

WE REGRET THAT SEASONAL MARINE LAYER CLOUD COVER OVER SOUTH-
ERN CALIFORNIA COASTLINE MADE IT IMPOSSIBLE TO OBTAIN
REQUESTED PICTURE OF MADONNA SUNBATHING TOPLESS IN MALIBU.

DOMICILE OF CLAUDIA SCHIFFER IN GERMANY IS SURROUNDED BY
DENSE TREES WHICH SERIOUSLY DEGRADE VISIBILITY DURING WARMER
SUMMER MONTHS WHEN SUBJECT IS LIKELY TO USE POOL.

WOMAN IN BIKINI IN 8 AUGUST PHOTOGRAPH OF SEN. ALFONSE D'AM-
ATO'S BACKYARD IN LONG ISLAND, NEW YORK, HAS BEEN IDENTIFIED
AS HIS SISTER, MARIA FONSECA. ALTHOUGH MS. FONSECA'S HAIR
APPEARS TO BE HER OWN, SHE IS IN FACT WEARING A WIG.

Affidavit

STATE OF ARKANSAS)
)SS
COUNTY OF PULASKI)

      The undersigned, Lambchop, hereby states on personal knowledge under oath and penalty of perjury:

      1.   That I am a hand puppet; that I am making this Affidavit of my own free will without duress, coercion or threats from others; and that I have not received nor have I been promised any future compensation for making this Affidavit.

      2.   That on May 7, 1991, I was appearing in a show at the Garland Theater in Little Rock, Arkansas, which concluded at approximately 8:45 P.M., at which time I was escorted to my dressing room by Shari Lewis.

      3.   That at approximately 9:00 P.M. a person identified as Arkansas State Trooper Ward Calhoun entered my dressing room and informed me that then Governor Bill Clinton wished to meet me in person, whereupon I decided to meet with him as requested.

      4.   That at approximately 9:15 P.M. the Governor entered my dressing room, placed me on his hand and proceeded to make me say dirty and disgusting things by the use of the techniques of ventriloquism, and while I was on his hand, scratched himself in a place I will not recount for the purposes of this affidavit.

      6.   That my encounter with the Governor caused, and continues to cause, embarrassment, shame, grief, horror, fright, worry, humiliation, and a pronounced unravelling of the threads around the bottom of my sock-like body.

      FURTHER AFFIANT SAYETH NOT.

Lambchop
_____
LAMBCHOP

SUBSCRIBED AND SWORN to before me this _____**6**th_____ day of July, 1996.

Patricia Brown
_____
NOTARY PUBLIC

Patricia Brown
Notary Public, State of Arkansas
No. 18-005551212
Qualified in Pulaski County
Commission Expires, May 31, 1997

Notes for possible kids book of nursery rhymes

(ask Chelsea what she thinks of idea)

Title: ~~IT TAKES A VILLAGE IDIOT~~
~~MOTHER HILLARY'S NURSERY RHYMES~~
A CHILD'S GARDEN OF EXCUSES

Concept: Teaches kids sometimes its okay to deny stuff if it might hurt someone (including yourself. Ha ha!)

Examples:

Jack and Jill went up the hill ~~to fetch~~ a pail of water
Jack fell down and broke his crown
But Jill could not recall
Either Jack's unfortunate fall
The climb, the hill, the pail, the spill, or any other matter.

Little Jack Horner sat in a corner eating his Christmas pie.
He put in his thumb, and pulled out a plum - an act he would later deny

Mary, Mary, quite contrary, how does your garden grow?
I think my staff planted tulips and daffs, but really I do not know.

Little Miss Muffet sat on a tuffet, eating her curds and whey
Along came a spider and sat down beside her and frightened Miss Muffet away.
Well, that's what Miss Muffet will say.
There wasn't a spider, she ate donuts with cider,
It just sounded better that way.

Mom - I don't think this is a real good idea. Why don't you write a legal thriller instead, like John Grisham? Or a Washington political novel. Honestly, the way those things are written, a sixteen year old kid could knock one out in a month. Chelsea ♡

RANDOM HOUSE

Royalty Department
201 East 50th Street
New York, NY 10023

STATEMENT #
1095-0118-01354

CONTRACT #
9501010

ACCOUNT #
0006754

TAX ID #
18-3299165

FOR THE ACCOUNT OF:
ANONYMOUS

TO:
DEE DEE MYERS MANAGEMENT
101 INDEPENDENCE AVE. SE
WASHINGTON, DC 20540

AUTHOR
CHELSEA CLINTON

TITLE
PRIMARY COLORS

ROYALTY STATEMENT SUMMARY
04/01/96 TO 09/30/96

	Net Units	Amount
OPENING BALANCE		($100,000)
CURRENT PERIOD CONTRACT EARNINGS FOR		
PRIMARY COLORS: PRIMARY COLORS		
ROYALTY ON SALES	1,325,876	$3,144,330
(DEDUCTIONS) FOR ADVANCE		($100,000)
(RESERVE AGAINST RETURNS)		($2,000,000)
CURRENT PERIOD CONTRACT BALANCE		$1,054,330
YOUR (DEDUCTIONS) & CREDITS BALANCE FROM PRIOR STATEMENT		.00
PAYMENT DUE ACCOUNT		$1,054,330

PLANS FOR SECOND TERM

- Fed program to place "Gideon" condoms in hotel room night tables right next to Bibles
- Put gays in space, on Supreme Court — everywhere
- Recognize Cuba — suck up to Castro — get in on ground floor of Cuban beachfront property
- Need easy military victory — invade Bahamas?
- Make Al D'Amato Ambassador to Mars (ha-ha!)
- Play more golf!

A John Boswell Associates Book

Produced by Patty Brown

Designed by Charles Kreloff

Calligraphy, Stamps, Original Artwork, and Really Nice Touches by Ron Barrett

Computer Imaging by John E. Barrett

Special Thanks to:
Anonymous, Jennifer Brown, Ward Calhoun, Amy Handy, Fernando Sarmiento, and the crew at Broadway Books, especially Lauren Marino and Kati Steele.

A Very Special Thanks to:
Broadway Books publisher, Bill Shinker, for coming to us with the idea and making this the first book on his first list.

Special Un-Thanks to:
The Microsoft Corporation, whose bug-laden and maddeningly incompatible Word 6.0 program made the production of this book an absolute nightmare.

Photography credits: Photograph of the Clinton family wearing duck hats, Sygma; photograph of Hillary Clinton used in Jane Fonda /Hanoi composite, Sygma; photograph of Bill and Hillary Clinton used in Mt. Rushmore composite, Allen Tannenbaum/Sygma; photograph of Elvis Presley, UPI/Corbis-Bettmann.

FIRST EDITION

ISBN 0-553-06763-X

96 97 98 99 00 10 9 8 7 6 5 4 3 2 1